A SUMMER STORY

Written and illustrated by K G Subramanyan

Seagull Books

CALCUTTA, 2019

First published in 1972 at the Fine Arts Fair
by the Graphic Art Department,
Faculty of Fine Arts, M. S. University of Baroda.

Seagull Books, 2008
Second printing, 2019

ISBN 978 8 1704 6 287 3

Published by Naveen Kishore
Seagull Books Private Limited
36C, S.P. Mukherjee Road, Calcutta 700 025

Typeset by Seagull Books, Calcutta, India
Printed and bound by Hyam Enterprises, Calcutta, India

July, but there was still no sign of rain.

Clouds crossed the sky but they only made the heat hotter.

I was thirsty.

But what could a crow like me
do on a day like this?

There was no water anywhere.
The wells were dry
and there were no waterholes.

I would have to fly miles and miles
to reach anywhere.
In this heat.

Unless I get to a town.
Crows know that, in times like this,
to go where men live is best

They put things by
when things are plenty
for days when they are scarce.

So I flew towards the nearest town over a dry and barren land.

When I reached there, it was noon.

The streets were empty.
The doors were barred.
The cisterns and horse-troughs were dry.

There was no water anywhere.

Except in a small bottle on a pushcart at the street corner. I thanked heaven for that.

But I had thanked too early. How was I going to get at the water in the bottle unless I could get my beak in?

My beak was too fat and neck of the bottle, too narrow.

So, as usual, I went to Grandpa for advice.
A doddering old crow he was, but he had seen the world.
And, often, had useful things to say.

Sure enough, he had a way.

Go and get pebbles
from the riverbed,
he said, and drop them in.

When they fill the bottle,
the water will come up to the brim
for pebbles and water
can't be in the same place.

This he'd learnt
from his old man.

And his old man had learnt it
from an old Greek crow
called Ar-crow-medes

That was great!

I didn't even wait to thank him.
Off I went to the riverbed
where pebbles there were
in all shapes and sizes.

Pebbles are tricky things
for crows to carry.

They slip out or slide in.
So I had to carry them carefully,
piece by piece.

On a day like this, it was not easy to do.
I panted and sweated
and the colour of my wings started to run.

And I grew thirstier each time.

So, on my last flight, I thought
I would carry two together.
But that wasn't easy to do either
for one would always slip away.

Still, I made an effort
and carried two some distance.

But, as luck would have it,
plop went one
on the glass roof of the greenhouse.

And clitter-clatter went the glass.

Not a great loss to me.

But, with a shudder came the thought
that I could break my bottle, too,
with such a pebble.
And Grandpa's trick may not work.

That made me mad.

I flew helter-skelter.

Until, suddenly, I noticed the poster over the bus stop.

To think that it had been there all the time
and I, like a fool, had never lifted my head to see it.

If men can drink through straws, then so can crows.
If they are clever.

Straws were plenty in the haystacks.

I drew a few out, clipped and cleaned them.

And used them the way men do.

I don't blame Grandpa, though.
He was wise in his own way.

But each age has its own bag of tricks.